Water Poems

Compiled by John Foster

Contents

Acknowledgements

The Editor and Publisher wish to thank the following who have kindly given permission for the use of copyright material:

David Andrews for 'It's raining out' © 1988 David Andrews; Eric Finney for 'The day the hose flipped' © 1993 Eric Finney; John Foster for 'Going for a swim' and 'The sea' both © 1993 John Foster; Tony Mitton for 'Without any water' © 1993 Tony Mitton; Ian Souter for 'The Great Water Giant' © 1993 Ian Souter; Jill Townsend for 'Water' © 1993 Jill Townsend.

It's raining out

'It's raining out,' said Mum to me,
'So don't forget your hat.
You're going to need your wellies, too.
You can't go out like that.'

I put my hat and wellies on
And went out in the rain.
I ran through puddles big and small
That I found down in the lane.

I went and shook the holly bush.
It dripped all over me.
I chased a frog down by the pond,
Then I went home for tea.

'Just look at you,' said Mum to me,
'You've ruined your nice new hat,
And got your wellies soaking wet.
You can't come in like that!'

David Andrews

The Great Water Giant

The Great Water Giant
has finished his bath.

He pulls the huge plug
out of the clouds.
He roars his thunderous laugh
and a wet, slippery waterfall
spills out of a squelchy sky.

'Look out below,' he seems to shout,
as the water

```
s           p           g
p           l           u
l     s     i     p     s     s
o     p     s     l     h     l
o     l     h     o     e     u
s     a     e     s     s     s
h     s     s     h           h
e     h     s     e           e
s     e           s           s
      s
```

and soaks deep into the thirsty earth.

Ian Souter

The day the hose flipped

'Right,' said Dad,
'I'll turn the hose on
Round the back.'
We were washing the car—
It was really black.

We waited a bit
Me and our Chris,
Then the water came through
With a noisy hiss.

6

The water came through
With a splutter and a gush,
It came bursting through
With a mighty rush.

And the hose came alive
Like a twisting snake.
It soaked Chris's jeans
As if he'd jumped in the lake.

7

It drenched my dress.
The hose still flipped about,
And next door's cat
Got a waterspout.

When Dad arrived back,
He said, 'Gosh!
It's *the car* that's supposed
To be getting a wash!'

Eric Finney

9

Going for a swim

On hot summer days, after school,
We go for a swim in the swimming pool.

As soon as I'm ready, I jump straight in.
I gasp as cold water splashes my skin.

I paddle across and cling to the side,
Then pull myself out to go on the slide.

I check that it's safe, then let myself go,
With a splash, I crash into the water below.

I go underwater, but I don't care.
I come to the surface for a breath of air.

Then I swim as fast as I can to the side
And I climb back up for another slide!

John Foster

The sea

The sea can be angry.
The sea can be rough.
The sea can be wild.
The sea can be tough.

The sea can rip.
The sea can tear.
The sea can roar
Like a hungry bear.

The sea can be gentle.
The sea can be flat.
The sea can be calm
As a sleeping cat.

The sea can glide
Over the sand,
Stroking the beach
Like a giant hand.

John Foster

Without any water

Without any water
there wouldn't be drinks.
There wouldn't be washing
and there wouldn't be sinks.

There wouldn't be rivers
and there wouldn't be seas.
There wouldn't be water
for plants and trees.

Without any water,
without a drop,
there would be no life
and the world would stop.

Tony Mitton

15

Water

It runs through your fingers,
it slides down your face,
it jumps from the shower
all over the place.

It bubbles in saucepans,
dives into your bath,
then goes down the drain
with a dirty laugh.

Jill Townsend